The Observer's World

Aayushi Laura

BookLeaf Publishing

India | USA | UK

Presentation by *BookLeaf Publishing*

Web: www.bookleafpub.com

E-mail: info@bookleafpub.com

ISBN: 9789363312074

First edition 2024

To the quiet observers of the world, who find beauty in the unnoticed and meaning in the mundane.

To the extraordinary children who dream big and strive tirelessly, whose hearts are both tender and resilient.

To the family and friends who support unconditionally, and to the strangers who leave lasting impressions.

And to all who read these words and see a reflection of their own journey.

This book is for you.

ACKNOWLEDGEMENT

Writing each poem has been a profound and long journey of two long years, and it would not have been possible without the support and encouragement of many remarkable individuals.

First and foremost, I extend my deepest gratitude to my mother, whose unwavering love and belief in me have been my greatest source of strength. Your constant support and understanding have allowed me to pursue my passion and pour my heart into these poems.

To my friend, thank you for your endless encouragement and for being my sounding board, my critic, and my cheerleader. Your honest feedback and genuine interest in my work have been invaluable.

I would also like to express my appreciation to all the people who have shaped me and transformed me into the person I am today. No matter how difficult or challenging our interactions may have been, you have all contributed to my life lessons and growth. Your influence has been an integral part of this journey, adding depth and complexity to my understanding of the world.

A special thank you to my readers, who have embraced my work with open hearts and minds. Your connection to these poems gives them life and meaning, and for that, I am profoundly grateful.

Lastly, to the countless moments of inspiration—the quiet observations, the fleeting emotions, and the cherished memories —that have fueled this collection, thank you. It is through these moments that 'The Observer's World' has come to life.

With heartfelt appreciation,
Aayushi

PREFACE

In the journey of life, we often find ourselves entangled in the web of memories, aspirations, and emotions that shape who we are. This collection of poems, 'The Observer's World', is a reflection of such a journey—one marked by the relentless pursuit of excellence, the tenderness of empathy, and the indelible imprints of a vivid past.

I have always strived for the extraordinary, setting high standards and pushing boundaries. Each poem in this book is a testament to the challenges, triumphs, and heartaches that accompany such a path. They are the echoes of an extraordinary child, whose curiosity and drive have been both a gift and a burden.

Empathy has been my constant companion, guiding me through the intricate dance of human interactions. Yet, with this quality comes a vulnerability—a susceptibility to the wounds that life inevitably inflicts. These poems are born from those moments where sensitivity has made the heartache but also deepened the understanding of what it means to be truly human.

In sharing these verses, I hope to offer solace and connection to those who find themselves on similar journeys. May you see your own reflections in these words and feel a sense of camaraderie in knowing that you are not alone in your experiences.

'The Observer's World' is not just a collection of poems; it is a mosaic of lived experiences, a tapestry woven with the threads of ambition, kindness, and resilience. I invite you to immerse yourself in these pages, to walk with me through the memories of the past and the dreams of the future.

Thank you for joining me on this poetic voyage.

With heartfelt sincerity,
Aayushi

CONTENTS

Once a Dreamer, Always a…?

Once a dreamer, I was extraordinary
In possession of more talents and charms.
"Only a few can reach my level," I told Maa.
Nineteen and lost,
Confidence fueled by ambitions utmost.
An imaginary land, what I did was just right.

Then failure tagged along,
Nerve wrecking, never-ending bitter failure.
Lost hope in what I could be,
Yet just as headstrong as I used to be,
Just as confident but a tad annoyed.
Anxious all the time yet confidence never left
my side.
Hence, I had to take a bigger L
Consecutive, bitter, never-ending failure.

Believe I was humbled down by time.
When did I become such a realist?
Guess we'll never find.
Was it time or was it me?
No human would ever mind.

Stringent Shot

Where do I stop?
Thought, it was a stringent shot.
All of them I find at the top
Time's going, clock's ticking
Can't wrap my head around it all.

Surrounded by echoing beats
Struggling to win. Oh! The wound of cheats.
A pawn, a spy, in the game of teenage rift
Where's my focus, God when did it shift?
They say, "kindness wins all sorts of hearts"
Took a blink, and got buried in the dirt.

A death wish for known strangers,
A cruel kiss for I faced all that danger.
Honey eclipse, sugar coats, sweet notes,
Stringent shots.
Oh! Why couldn't I ever connect the dots?
One glimpse, just a sight, leading life as a riot.

Where did I learn all that?
A lie, two lies, an old friend was a spy
Sold my soul; a relentless cry.

Thought, I was a crimson clover.
All watched, watched me as my game got over.

Forbidden Tryst

Hush! Don't cry out loud now, about
the unraveling tale of your dark days.
An accomplice's trust is all she needs
But really, isn't that her greed?

Never forgo the stories that they can't bear
Poor scarred soul, just wanted him to hear.
So the folktales and the legends pass on,
Untangling a forbidden tryst.
Isn't it what they all said about their clandestine
drift?

So, she dwells in darkness unknown,
Never seeking solace in audiences known.
Only to get stigmatized, polarized,
Poor soul, seeks no paradise.

Sacrificed to rituals, just to be born again?
All watched her with mirth, as she
Clinged to the last twig of a decaying tree,
Must have really wanted to be free.

Nostalgia

Trickling effect, I see rainbow lids
Soaking in liquid my iris scarcely find
Numb is the feeling, dumb my brain.

My soul reeks of a boy
Only through my eyes in vain.
Broken down like a Chinese toy.

Hurt so deep, past profound
No amount of words could ever be found.
Wasn't it bound?

What is it that you crave the most?
Nostalgia. Him. An unknown coast.

Karma

Achieve greatness, but at what cost?
What about all the people you have lost?
Heard you put a dagger in people's back,
Twisting it harder, relentlessly getting dragged.
Working hard, they do expect,
But when does it end?
Where's your karma? You must get.
You, definitely not the type that karma forgets.

Greatness usually remains unseen
or unheard, if not done with bliss in mind.
Oh! She was chaotically one of a kind.
Yet she bleeds from the knife of her fate
Karma I suppose, wasn't her greatest mate.

Bygones Be Bygones

Wish you were here but you're not,
How to pinpoint? It's just not a dot.
Had hoped for a better future,
But none of them could be here.
Left as I led the way,
Hope to see y'all again someday.
Dreamt of a life filled with love and light.
All left, left me without a fight.

Some only cared cause I had the riches,
Few stayed, we hated the same b'tches.
In the battlefield bruised and bled, got numerous
stitches.
Failed to preach endless speeches.
Left as I led the way,
Never wish to meet y'all again someday.

A Renegade

I know now where it came from,
Amongst the pits of my darkest dreams.
As if almost a nightmare
Nothing, not even a thing was fair.

The alms or psalms, nothing to relish
My hopes and dreams all vanished.
For him, or her, or anyone,
How could it ever be?
No one to checkmate; Lord, make me free.

But I know not where it came from;
That damn dagger…
Always with a fresh drop of my blood on it.
Definitely wasn't carved out of a tree.
Not so long ago, neatly drawn on my back
God, how could she?

It hurts me so as I long for a woundless back,
Their stealthy moves, still deteriorating my
health.
The dagger? I know not.
"But it was never about you"
Oh! These voices in my head…

No traces, no wounds
No evidence in sight.
I gave up; it was never a fair fight.
Wonder if it will always be about me…
How neatly all their moves were made,
No one to talk to, just knew they wouldn't even
care.

Oh! How I go on and on and on about it.
The Great Betrayal…
I never escaped.
My beloved, no name, a *Renegade*.

The Unsung Song

In shadowed notes, where echoes sigh,
Melody draped in somber skies.
Minor chords whisper tales untold,
A haunting tune, mind's grip on hold.

Strings of sorrow, a piano's lament,
Each note a tear, my heart's descent.
Echoes of pain, rhythms do embrace,
Symphonies of melancholy, a destitute space.

Drums beat often, like a weary heart,
Aching lyrics tearing my soul apart.
In distressing tunes, emotions unfold,
A song of despair, a story untold.

Debacle

Bittersweet failure,
How do I acknowledge you?
Should I thank you
for teaching me the most important lesson?
Or should I regret having ever known you?

You are the most painful feeling
You take my hopes and dreams
a step further away from me.
Don't understand
How would I ever acknowledge you…
Do me a favor, Oh! Bittersweet failure.

Give me some rest for I am tired
Any ounce more of you is not my desire.
Let me sleep. Oh fear!
Let the winters passby
For I am spring's dear.
Let me sleep. Oh fear!

Despair

No solace found my sibling distant roam,
in solitude's embrace longing for home.
Neither refuge in bonds nor trust be found,
echoes of loneliness haunts me down.
A heart, so shattered lays on the ground,
despaired darkness knows no bounds.

Aporia

What happened that led me to this fate?
Was I not careful enough?
How certain events took place,
What have I missed amidst it all?
Did I not see signs all this time?
Am I not capable enough?
Why didn't I think it through?
The knot in my head can't be untangled yet.

Utopia

Dreamt of a faraway land,
It had some sort of freedom in the air.
Would fly there; and be happy - quite a simple
plan.
The freshness of Carnations would blow through
my hair.

Nostalgia surrounds me, as I sit
and dream of this unbeknownst place.
Should I take my Mother with me or should I
travel alone?
What could have been…
Don't have the courage to know.
Yet I miss that fairyland so dearly,
Still wonder what could have been if only I
went.

The War

All is right in the world.
Just a couple of thousand people dying in a
stupid war.
A few thousand kids losing their parents
A question - Will it ever be the same as before?
Alarmed bombing, squeaks of liberty
Not a clue what move to make
Nations United, heh! what a fake.

God's in heaven and everything's alright
Just a bunch of innocent humans losing their
lives.
Liberals and atheists, all alike
Preaching freedom into dark light.
Thrashing women and children;
Journalists do fight.

Whoever reports it, loses their right.
People commenting, bluntly picking sides
Well, this is just a minor highlight.
God's in heaven and everything else seems
alright.

Decisions Decisions

Skipped some important events
In the hope that I might not end
Empty stomach, broken on the streets.
It hurts me so to think, I might
be fine if there's no light.

In this plight, certain relationships I mend,
Let go of certain people, some I defend.
Analyzing the time-cost benefit of every move I
make,
Urgency and emergency, something I casually
fake.

Breaking hearts as I move on
This poor soul has been aching for so long.
Foes might not be speculating a new dawn,
Time is what makes us its pawn.

Contrarian Bliss

It turned into something bigger,
Somewhere somehow I got a sense
of betrayal.
My friends, fam and foes,
All in all, sense and feelings lingers,
Heart skips a beat, breathing flickers.
Frozen grounds, feisty rounds,
They say it is a contrarian bliss.

The mind makes up yet another sh't.
Bleeding scars and empty skies,
Crossing borders, breaking ties.
Increased palpitations with watery eyes,
Still chasing stars on blurry nights.
My mind yearns for whatever's worth,
Everything around was a mirth.

"Amongst the angst of it all
You've been hurt
Unaware who did that to your heart…"
Wrote my mind, they bought it out,
Yet the book was never sold.
Lessons from this chapter will never get old.
"Let it be. Let it go" they told.

Anxious mind seldom triggers,
No warning signs, just crazy lines.
A constant haunting sound,
Cause you never got to keep your ground.

Moon Child

Child of the cosmos, may you roar high as tides
Limitless as the sky, scary as the night.
You suffered much, only to be free
Moonlight awakens the quietest of the seas.
Look at the sky, look at the stars in your eyes.

You were born from & will end in dust
Your knowledge is the only thing that wouldn't
ever rust.
May you endure the pain,
Enjoy as you endure.
Feel the selene, she would always lure.

Anguish or Agony

As each day passes by
Few of my brain cells die.

Every single day that I spend in sorrow
How I always hope for a better tomorrow.

I live in the past they say
Can't really comprehend my decay.

Nostalgia hits me more often
Blurry memories in retro reels
Makes me wonder what is it that I truly feel.

Can neither explain nor complain
Want to scream and wish to share
But no one's really here.

The endless pain,
Anguish and Agony
Or whatever it is that means the same.
Better tomorrow? Pray.

As I Compose

Silently I cry, composing a musing
Teardrops and words, rarely of my choosing.
More often than other people can take
My delusional brain tells me they fake
The emotion that a poet requires.
Empathy, experience, and pain,
Madness, sin and the feeling of disdain.

So out of touch, losing all I gain
One more tear falls, yet again.
A grudge in the poet's mind hardly dies
More drops fall from my soaked brown eyes.
Heart is heavy, pulse runs fast
When will it all end? Help, I am lost.

Delulu

Harshly struggling but so are you
It is hard to figure out which is worse?
Analyzing life is off the charts
Game of survival, that's how it starts.
Existential distress wrecks us out
With every passing second kicks in self-doubt.

I try and I try
To keep my composure as I soothe you
Too soft for the world yet I fight to keep us new.
Deviated, silently screaming out loud
Every passing minute increases self-doubt.

Turned around, and no one's happy
Perceived people, profoundly empty.
Like a vessel that was bound to sink
'Titanic' was merely a sob story they think.

Clear skies are followed by dark nights.
Try not to fade, might even win the fight.
What is it? Where are we headed?
Delusion is not the solution!
"In the end, it all begins."

Stand solid and face the repulsion.
It takes more than just winds to finish an
excursion.

The Great Betrayal

Scrolling through the pictures,
I had once saved on my computer,
With much anticipation.
Know not yet, what sort was I
a key person?

I made you my mural,
looked up to you in the sky.

Bigger than the whole world,
We traversed as we grew old.
Never went that far with anybody else,
Never trusted anyone more than myself.

Heard you accomplished the American dream,
Yet your wishes resemble that of a teen.
Oh! How loud could you scream?
Crucified me whilst I played on your team.

How's the dagger in my back doing now?
Have I stopped bleeding yet?
Did you find new alchemy somehow?
Would burn down my house, I bet.

The stardust and pixie glitter
The dress, the shoes, and the glam
All that you ever gave me,
Was thrown away by this lone hand.

I painted you so big,
Bigger than it gets as I entailed you into poetry.
But you schemed plots around my neck,
Snapped it all at once,
I struggled for the last breath.

Oh, What the heck!
Just like that, you lost all respect,
What on earth did I even get?
The great betrayal.

Liberty-Shiberty

What is this feeling?
Can someone explain…
Half a decade went
Liberated, only yesterday I felt.

"Liberty-shiberty is all fine
What about the anxiety underlying?
Hate to admit
Can't catch a break
Writing long letters
Only to fake
Emotions, and all sorts of crap
Why is life such a trap?"

Failed to elaborate so I kept it short
Writing long emails, only to send a note.
Can someone help me? I am lost.
Kind sir, please elaborate - Why did you ghost?

"I'm sorry but you've got the wrong address it
seems.
Your poetry sure does rhyme
Not quite sure if it's worth a dime."

"But please tell me what my feelings mean,
Am I ever going to get well?"

"It really is hard to tell,
You took a long shot, so you fell."

To Do And To Be

Thinking of things I ought to be
Learning, processing all at once.

Her senses are better than mine
His paintings are one of a kind.

I sing, I write; I draw, and I paint
Learning everything from scratch.

Yet, I still remain the same,
A hard ball to catch.

Heard someone call out my name
What is her wicked game?

I try and I try
And continue to fail.

Heard it all, knew nothing but my own soul.
I oughta be a fighter, a writer
A kindred soul, someone who achieved her goal.
Composing songs is what I do all day long; sing along.

On Her Having Arrived At The Age Of Twenty-Three

The subtle thief — time
Has stolen my three and twentieth year!
Passing the days sublime as I fail to find a
career,
Late spring, am I to wait in line?
My semblance does deceive the truth
That I to womanhood am so near;
Sophistication and maturity much less appear,
Not to forget the frightened youth.

Be it quiet or bustling, quick or slow,
In cosmic dance where hopes are chosen
As my mind currents flow,
Fate approaches heaven, as such my dreams are
woven,
All is, if I have the courage to show,
In grandeur, fates intertwine and grow.

A Thin Line

Craving sweet rest
When would this weight lift off my chest?
Decades of hurt I carry within
The line between Freedom & Bondage,
Oh, so thin!

Mental Pressure above the sky
Wings torn, might never fly.
He says that he knows my tactics all too well
This house he made, I hardly ever dwell.

Claiming to never have stopped me
Whatever I am or am supposed to be.
Dark visions of the ocean and the sea,
Lay me down, set me free.

Child Within

Found a body,
a broken heart,
a shattered soul,
Yet found nothing at all.

Expected to mature,
Act mature, talk mature.
Punished for things,
reasonable to the beings.

It was the same,
never wanted change.
Wanted peace.
Wanted his mom to tell him he was not wrong.

Yet the child died an excruciatingly painful
death,
wanted to save it but was struggling to catch my
own breath.

To save it, nurture it apparently
but the bullet had left the barrel silently.
It was gone. Brutally killed.
It died a slow death and took a part of me
along as it left.

Solace

Poetry. It brings me peace
Rests my heart
Gives me the strength I need.

Calms me down, eases my soul
Takes me to the shore
As I sink singing 'Folklore'
Faded light finds some hope.

Anxiety diminishing
Ego swinging
Everything is a little less vague
Just because I found solace.

Introspection

I knew a boy once so gentle and soft
One of a kind, truly a mama's boy
His mom loved him just a tad more than
She loved her daughter.
Enjoyed riding horses together
And played football on hot summer days.

Sought in him the love she never received
From her husband or her family.
Knew she raised an honest boy
In front of all, subtly coy.

Sensitive chap, constantly mellow,
Much different from all the other fellows.
Bullied, sullied, and all that stuff
His purity was what distinguished him
The line mother drew was partly thin.

I hate that I hurt him at times
"But I am his sister"; for every time
I say this, wish I had a nickel or a dime.
Tad jealous, a tad angry, and always acting right.

In this journey gave him a thorough fight.
But he was so pure, so sweet
And I, just a wannabe.

Never ceasing to be covetous,
His integrity I reckoned tremendous.
No wonder, Mother did the right thing
She chose the right being.

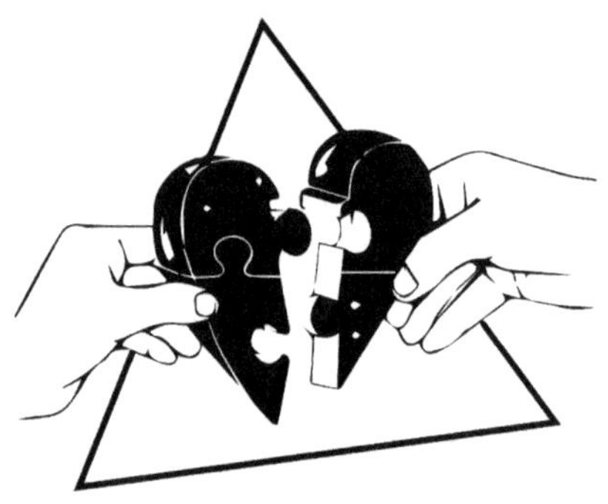

Unmendable

Children often forget the disappointment of the
previous years,
the scandal, the drama that they witnessed
during one of their visits to the relatives,
they indulge with cousins with the same
enthusiasm
and again the excursion ends up being an
inevitable disappointment,
they come back home as a victim, a sob-sob
story haunts them for days
yet once again the year passes by and they forget
their past disappointments,
the enthusiasm for the excursion repeats in
circles.

Until it stops.
Continuing to haunt them forever.
Relationships once tainted become unmendable.
Parents on such occasions are commendable.
Sometimes it's the arrogance of the child.
Some other, pity of parents towards the child.
Conclusively the child suffers.
One day, he refuses to buffer.
Then they all say "What a pity he couldn't join
us today."

Voids

Voices supersedes my dark voids,
As the full moon raises high tides.
Juggling my senses as I struggle to thrive,
Consequently, a fool might not strive.

Felt alright when I woke up,
Was doing almost fine at dawn.
Void emerged with the approaching midnight,
Who cares? Who even wants to fight?

Unexplainable. Unimaginable.
Crucially coaxing light.
Undependable. Undesirable.
Unavoidable void of night.

Mi Madre

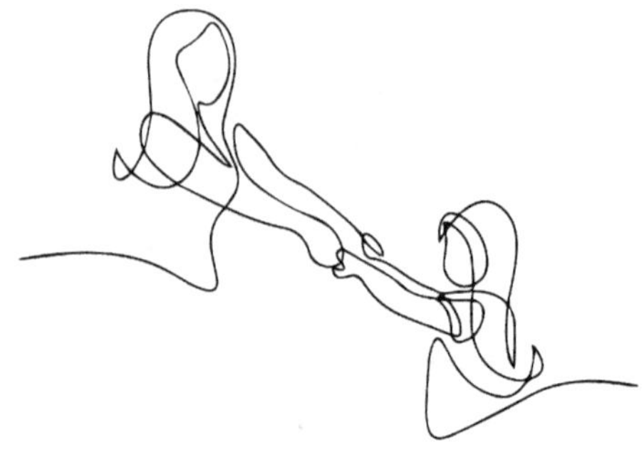

Miraculously we became best friends
Can't pinpoint how it began
Told her tonight about a struggling stance.

Listened to me tensely
For a moment there
Almost forgot who she was
As if I was talking to an angel
Enjoying while it lasts.

She did give me some solid advice
In that moment she sure was right.
Well, I wonder if she's ever been wrong
For her, I would write a thousand more songs.

Where There Is Light...

45

In darkness, I went after the light
In light, my shadow followed me.

Immortalizing My Sincerity

My mural, my muse
A canon, everything but old news.
There will be a time
We will cease to be.

But there will be our fragments
Cause I plan to immortalize you.
With a picturesque image, there ever was
And a song composed in the sweetest melody.

Stories written of your valor,
Paint on my cheeks of your color.
How you carved the path that led to me
Only so we could be.

Commemorating our greatest memories
Our clandestine affair,
A home we once shared.

A truce, my muse,
Anything but old news.
I wish to immortalize you.

A Tear

The yearning and longing
of my sweet childhood belonging
of not just me but us both.
The dreams and the chaos
Seldom got written.

It passed slowly in phases,
Watched a house being built.
We did dodge several pitfalls,
The stairs and the cases
But we could never build a wall.

Could never fly a kite
or strike the right chords of a guitar,
Until one fine day, you went a bit far.
Met you on lunch breaks every day
Realizing you were a bit ashamed of my
Poking, teasing, and constant appeasing.

Nostalgic or haunting I know not yet.
Our hopes or dreams or secrets no longer
intersect.
Flew to a land down below, you know I always
did suspect.

Tonight, missing you, I shed a tear.
Want to go to bed,
But oh! The bloodbath and battles I fear.
Want to sleep tight,
But oh! The nightmares.

Ashes to the ground

Grey skies overhead, we reached the terrace.
"Bring out the stuff before water touches the
ground,
None of it should ever be found."
Notes, letters, and memos known
"Burn them to the ground, to each his own."

All the papers he had kept hidden for long,
The girl he knew, who loved him all along.
Failing to burn the matchsticks
Never had been this enthusiastic.
We laughed through our tears.
"No one can see these", kicks in worst fear.

Tiny raindrops splash on my cheek
"I saw someone there, he took a peak."
"Hurry up" he panicked, "there's much left to set
afire."

Bring out the lighter, buckle up fighter.
In worry and hurry, we set them ablaze.
Half-burned pages hit their way,
they touched the ground, we turned around.
Scared if they would ever be found.

"The rain will soak our pasts profound."
It had been charming,
was quite warming.
We set our feet astray,
Some stories should never find their way.

Frailty

From where do my insecurities arise?
Have I lost faith in myself,
Maybe I should just close my eyes.
I try and I try to forgive myself
Forgive him, forget everyone else.

But how miserably I fail so...
Falling down bruising my knees
Visions of the past blur my judgment as I go.

Maybe his heart has a different set of keys
Things in the morning look swell.
Night appears with blackness of some sort
Lingering anxiety, hearts in darkness dwell.
If only confrontations weren't my last resort
Maybe then, I would have had him at all costs.

Reminiscing

The greens, blues, yellows and red
All are beginning to mess with my head.
Numerous sorrows and tears to hide
Crippling anxiety with rules to abide.

But what went wrong, my dear?
Years and years of baggage, I fear.
Loaded on my innocent shoulders.
Matured too soon,
More responsible than the responsibilities I had.

Playful; Youthful childhood,
Oh! My long lost childhood.
How do I ask you to come back?
The load has begun to attack.

He Said, She Said

On a chilly winter eve,
He calls and yells,
"Yet again did you ring my cell?"
Too stunned to speak, what a toll on my head.
Want to clear the air
Yet screamingly says, "Go to hell".

The pretenders and pathological liars
The kings and queens of manipulations
Yet again point the gun toward me
A child at heart, my world a chaos it seems.

Now and then I look back and reflect
On the darkest days of my teenage thrill
Never caught up yet again on
What he said, she said.

Such a bliss it turned out to be
To have no mutual friends
No nerve to ever strike.
No loser in the fight.

Sin

Is it a sin to please,
Doing things you don't appease?
The mechanics, the components,
The functional flaws.
Could never comprehend how to...
Probably never will.
Mama told me it is evil.
So, I nod along and remain tense
Interesting influence indeed
When does it end?

On Mother's Day

When we were young, little kids
You told us we could rule the world.
So we put on our capes to play pretend,
Wish I could relive every single word.
We grew up and led different paths,
might never cross, but your aging ground,
most certainly a dreadful loss.
Through thick and thin and all that chaos,
You tell us we could still have it all.

Mother, laid our foundation oh! so strong,
Never let us take a hit, always stood along.
Held our hands under the greyest of skies,
Him & I, too strong to ever defy.

Bold somehow, something inevitably sharp
Some hard papers, a few relations went dark.
Whirlwind of cheats, still even dread,
Schemes and plots of all that's left unsaid.
Never stood a chance to rift us apart,
Yet again, Mother, I was just playing my part.

Spirits high in my castle of cinder block,
Strong arsenal, my Mother a solid rock.

Altruism

Known real love;
It has four legs and a wagging tail.
Trust profound, a prolonged wail,
In its presence, worries grow pale.
Every glance, a heartfelt tale,
Together, through every trail.

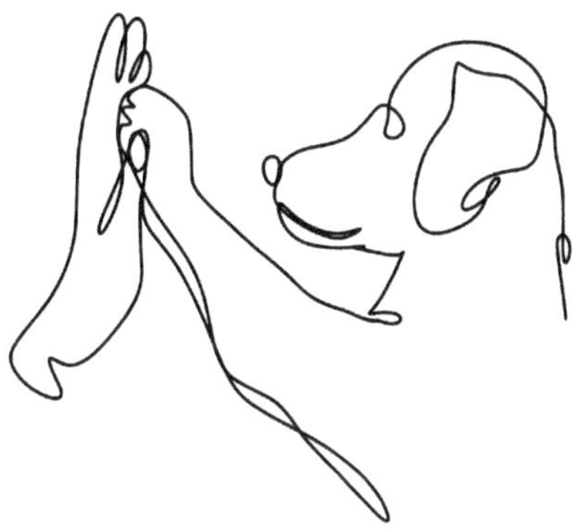

The Rollout

So the world turned against me,
I wasn't afraid anymore,
But that's not how the world works,
Self-destruction was self-inflicted after all.

Fit In

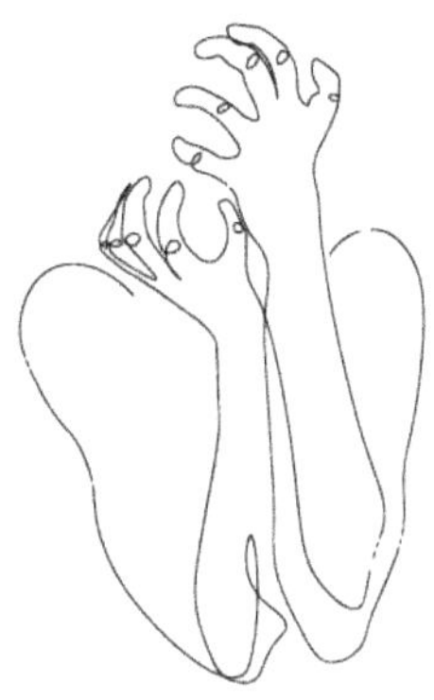

Coping to fit in, her body aches
Soul longs for home, not the place,
She once knew as a child —
The one that gives rest to the mind.
Failing to find,
Yearns for the peace that comes along.
Two houses, none to own.
Straying thoughts all night long.
Wandering mind finds no ease,
So long, till soul appease.

Where to go? What to do?
None to follow, Some to lose.

The Egoist

"What is it that you've achieved?
You're not even that good..." said the cheat.
Bipolar; methinks.
At times, loving and caring.
At times, a freak.

Could sue you, if you ever cross her path.
What's the difference between her and a
sociopath?
Respect is earned,
A lesson she never learned.

Sits on the seat as if she's never known defeat.
Everyone touch the ground; come lick her feet.
How come her ego never left?
How come her actions have known no effect?
Don't think that's her greed.
She is someone, one might always need.
Bipolar; indeed.

Accomplishing what others could never.
The pennies you made, may not last forever.
Monetary values earned,
Not a single lesson learned.
Declared she has the biggest heart,

Yet drifted lovers apart.
Wretched woman,
Even denies having played a part.

How is it that you never learned?
The Egoist, a bridge I burned.

Troubadour

Someday I wish to be a poem,
Will I ever get to be someone's muse?
For now, all I am is a poet.
Traditionally believed, modernly ignored,
The best sort of poet hardly gets bored.
Only with his perspicacity,
A poet writes to the best of his capacity.

Age Is Just A Number

Too blue to even begin,
The whole belief system has got to change.
Will I ever survive this,
Or sink in my own tears?
The misery is surreal,
It's just the age I fear.
Lost most of my friends this past year
And companions in one single blow.
Mom exclaimed, "That's just how you grow!"

Will I stand the test of time?
Will I ever cross the line?
The fear, The trauma, The anxiety surreal
How did I even get here?

Was only required to grow old
How the hell was I never bold?
Am I the first one to be this naive,
Will this blue ever become mauve?

Weed

You are growing like a weed on me
In the garden of my reverie.
Contemplating life makes me too sad
Yearning for the joy I once had.
On quiet nights society turns mad.
Pining to be free,
The weight of this world crashing over me.

Educated Goblins

Behind her back, all of them laughed
Poked her just for fun.
Wreckless kid just ran wild
Was nicknamed as 'that teacher's child'.
For the slightest of while, a bewildered smile.

Jealous much for all the logos?
Earned good money, remotely funny.
But what's the use?
When this is the life that she chose.
Pittiest leagues, gut-wrenching yields,
Digging the ground for the gold.

Couldn't even teach,
Mindless hollow preach.
Faced threats from many kids.
Trying to look better, ruthless chatter
Used locks on the loo's door.

Pettiness peaked, endless leagues
Would never admit fatigue.
As cheap as it gets, trying to take a drag.
Diamondless rings, their ego swings
In their heads, they're queens and kings.
No tinge of realization.

Students; always at the end of their accusation.
Gaslighting with endless screeching
From the state, constantly leaching.
Not half as good at teaching.

Not a drop of shame,
Still want to sit in the hall of fame.
Shattering students like glasses,
Losing interest in attending classes.
Must be having happy husbands at least?
Not a clue.
Ruthlessly sticking to the bills with the glue.

"Your skirt's too short,
let me leave your parents a note."
Perfect for the bins, so I labeled them 'Goblins'.
Wobbling all the easy money they earn.
Am sure that they'll never learn.

Incognito

Her head high in the sky
Personal life, she spells like a tale.
Her glory and valor, gossip turned pale.

"How many souls did you shatter?
Have you announced in the room,
How do you not know this girl you've groomed?
Have the parents called you yet?
You're yet to meet Karma, I suspect."

Portrays herself as an attentive reader,
Pretentious pawn trying to be a leader.
I, merely a fool demanding Poetic Justice
from someone who only knew Drama.
Waiting patiently for her to meet Karma.
How will she ever know what mental rust is?

"Did you get picked yet?
Did you meet death at your doorstep?"

Wrecking and ruining lives as she goes
Sincerity and dignity, terms she would never
know.
A good competition to Dolores Umbridge,
The gap between us, she could never bridge.

"No need to return the book you once lent,
My ego to the sky that day went."
Comprehensively not a saint;
With the color Black, you — I paint.

The Valley

Nestled in the embrace of emerald hills,
The valley whispers tales of serenity and peace.
The mist-kissed mornings, where sunlight gently
spills,
Unveil a symphony of nature's tender bliss.

Colonial echoes blend with modern rhythms,
Symphony of history and future's prism,
Crafting a tapestry of timeless ease.

Streams weave through the valleys,
Stories linger in hidden alleys.
A tranquil haven of time and space,
Where lovers' tender whispers leave a trace.

Wish I could linger there forever
In the serene realm, even the fox wasn't as
clever.

To never return, just bask in the glow,
Of happiness found in valleys below.
Every passing minute, a treasure to keep,
In Dehradun's arms, my soul does sleep.

To The Sea, Sincerely.

Once got lost on the coast of the Aegean Sea,
As in the wildest imaginations I had once dreamt
to be.
Never so serene and sincere I felt
Lost at the sea, my heart did melt.

Wandering beneath the cloudless skies
Salt streams passing down my blurry eyes.
The coast of my dreams, planes flying overhead
Arms wide open. Dear Sea,
show me your depth.

How moats and boats made me feel,
How cheap for that amount of thrill.

Only if I could get lost once again
Aegean Sea, Arabian Sea, or near Lombok
Strait,
never to be found the same.

The Land had always repulsed me,
Fearsome Sea, be kind, engulf me.

Bid 'The Observer' Farewell

Observing she went,
In front of others, she would never rant.
Escaping the mayhem, opened her notes.
Penning down all her thoughts.
Havoc on Earth was brought but she fiercely
wrote.

Poured her heart, only for some to note.
But no one cared, thoughts were never shared.
Observing she moved on,
From place to place, a lyricist born.

If not you, who is bound to ace?
Only you were acquainted with such grace.
Be quiet. Learn to hide.
Mean remarks. Coarsely snide.

Be quiet and *observe*. Don't argue.
These words you've befriended,
Will always find you.

9 789363 312074